IMPERFECTION ILLUMINATED:
UNVEILING JAPANESE WISDOM FOR A BALANCED LIFE

ASTRID AUXIER

© 2023 GENESEE WATCH CO (GWC)

First published in English in 2023 By Genesee Watch Co (GWC)

Copyright for the first English edition © 2023 Genesee Watch Co (GWC)

Title: Imperfection Illuminated: Unveiling Japanese Wisdom for a Balanced Life
Author: Astrid Auxier
Editor: A. Chan
Cover Design: Álvaro Oliveira For GWC
Graphic Design: Álvaro Oliveira For GWC
Layout: Perserose Catalan for GWC
Site: www.geneseewatch.com

ISBN: 978-1-954145-46-7

All rights reserved. No part of this publication may be reproduced, stored in a retrieval system, or transmitted in any form or by any means, electronic, mechanical, photocopying, recording, or otherwise, without the prior written permission of the publisher.

The author has made every effort to ensure the accuracy of the information provided in this book. However, neither the publisher nor the authors can be held responsible for any errors or omissions that may occur. The publisher also disclaims any responsibility for the content found on author or third-party websites.

> As the author, I would like to disclose that I utilize AI tools to assist in the editing and improvement of my writing. To enhance the quality and readability of my work, I utilized AI tools, including editing, grammar, and spell-checks. While these tools contribute to refining the content, it is important to note that no automated system is flawless. As a result, I strive to ensure the accuracy and clarity of my writing, but it is always recommended that readers exercise their own judgment and critical thinking. I am committed to delivering the best possible reading experience and appreciate your understanding and support.

table of contents

INTRODUCTION — 10

12
CHAPTER 01
Introducing Japanese Philosophies

16
CHAPTER 02
The Significance of Wabi-Sabi, Kaizen, and Ikigai in Japanese Culture

22
CHAPTER 03
The Benefits of Adopting These Philosophies in Daily Life

PART I: WABI-SABI – THE BEAUTY OF IMPERFECTION — 28

30  ## CHAPTER 04
From Zen Buddhism to Tea Ceremonies: A Brief History of Wabi-Sabi Aesthetics

34  ## CHAPTER 05
Core principles of Wabi-Sabi: Imperfection, Incompleteness, Impermanence

38  ## CHAPTER 06
Wabi-Sabi Everyday in Art, Design, and Architecture

42  ## CHAPTER 07
Mindfulness and Acceptance of Life's Imperfections

46  ## CHAPTER 08
Incorporating Wabi-Sabi into Personal Growth

PART II: KAIZEN – THE ART OF CONTINUOUS IMPROVEMENT

52

CHAPTER 09
The Origins and History of Kaizen

56

CHAPTER 10
The Post-World War II Japanese Economic Miracle

60

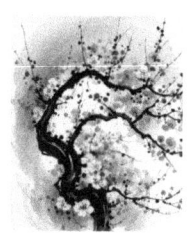

CHAPTER 11
The Role of Kaizen in Japanese Industries

66

CHAPTER 12
Core principles of Kaizen

70

CHAPTER 13
The PDCA Cycle and the 5S Methodology

76  **CHAPTER 14**
Kaizen in Everyday Life

80  **CHAPTER 15**
Implementing Kaizen in Work and Professional Growth

86  **CHAPTER 16**
Kaizen in Relationships and Communication

PART III: IKIGAI – THE REASON FOR BEING   92

94  **CHAPTER 17**
The Origins and History of Ikigai

100  **CHAPTER 18**
The Concept of Ikigai in Okinawan Culture

106  **CHAPTER 19**
The Four Pillars of Ikigai: Passion, Mission, Vocation, and Profession

112  **CHAPTER 20**
Discovering Your Ikigai

CONCLUSION 118

120  The Interconnectedness of Wabi-Sabi, Kaizen, and Ikigai

122  The Impact of Embracing These Philosophies on Overall Well-Being

124  A Call to Action: Integrating Wabi-Sabi, Kaizen, and Ikigai Into Daily Life for a More Fulfilled, Meaningful Existence

APPENDICES 128

130 Glossary of Japanese Terms

136 Bonus Tips for Incorporating Wabi-Sabi, Kaizen, and Ikigai Into Daily Routines

CHAPTER

01

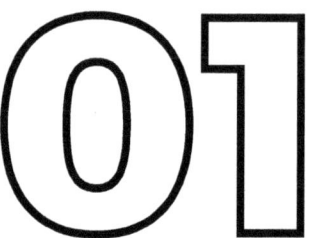

Introducing Japanese Philosophies

As I sit here in my study, surrounded by the countless books and scrolls that have been my constant companions for the past 30 years, I cannot help but reflect on my journey through the world of Japanese philosophies. It was a cold winter day in Kyoto when I first encountered the concept of Wabi-Sabi at a traditional tea ceremony. The warmth of the tea contrasted with the biting cold outside. Yet, I felt a strange sense of serenity and acceptance of the imperfections in life.

Throughout the years, my exploration of Japanese thought has led me to uncover the deep interconnectedness between the philosophies that permeate this beautiful culture. Japan, with its rich history and unique perspective on the world, has given birth to concepts like Wabi-Sabi, Kaizen, and Ikigai, which can not only enhance our understanding of Japanese culture but can also enrich our lives in profound ways.

My first encounter with Kaizen came during a visit to a Toyota factory. I marveled at how the employees, from management to assembly line workers, were constantly striving for improvement, no matter how small. This desire for continuous betterment resonated with me, and I felt compelled to apply the principles of Kaizen to my own life and work.

In an unexpected and life-altering way, the Japanese concept of Ikigai, which focuses on uncovering one's true purpose, found its way into my life. Following the loss of a dear friend, I sought comfort in introspection, contemplating my purpose, passions, and the elements that genuinely infused my life with meaning. It was during this period of deep reflection that I started to intricately interlace the principles of Ikigai into the fabric of my everyday existence.

As we delve deeper into these Japanese philosophies, it is important to recognize that they are not disparate, isolated concepts. Instead, they are intricately connected, each one offering unique insights and approaches to understanding the human condition.

This chapter serves as an introduction to these philosophies, providing the foundation for the rest of our journey together.

Wabi-Sabi, the beauty of imperfection, has its roots in Zen Buddhism and the tea ceremony. It is a celebration of the transience and flaws of the natural world, encouraging us to find beauty in the impermanent, incomplete, and imperfect. By embracing Wabi-Sabi, we learn to relinquish our attachments to perfection and appreciate life's simple, authentic splendor.

Kaizen, the art of continuous improvement, is a philosophy that has played a crucial role in Japan's post-World War II economic growth. Originally applied in the industrial sector, Kaizen has since expanded to include personal development, relationships, and communication. The practice of Kaizen teaches us that change and improvement are not one-time events, but rather an ongoing process of reflection, action, and growth.

Ikigai, the reason for being, is a concept that encourages us to find our true purpose in life. By identifying our passions, missions, vocations, and professions, we can uncover the unique convergence of elements that give our lives meaning and satisfaction. Cultivating our Ikigai allows us to lead a more fulfilled and content existence.

As we embark on this exploration of Japanese philosophies, I invite you to join me in opening your heart and mind to the wisdom of Wabi-Sabi, Kaizen, and Ikigai. Together, we will discover how these concepts can inspire us to lead richer, more meaningful lives as we learn to embrace imperfection, pursue continuous growth, and uncover our true purpose.

CHAPTER 02

The Significance of Wabi-Sabi, Kaizen, and Ikigai in Japanese Culture

As I strolled through the ancient streets of Kyoto, with their narrow alleys and traditional wooden homes, I was reminded of the deep connection between Japanese culture and the philosophies of Wabi-Sabi, Kaizen, and Ikigai. The whispers of history echoed through the air, carrying the wisdom of a people who have embraced these concepts for centuries.

Wabi-Sabi, Kaizen, and Ikigai are not just abstract ideas, but rather, they are interwoven into the very fabric of Japanese society. In this chapter, I will share with you some personal experiences and reflections on how these philosophies have permeated various aspects of Japanese culture and daily life.

Wabi-Sabi is a philosophy that has greatly influenced Japanese art, architecture, and design. I recall visiting the Katsura Imperial Villa, where I marveled at the simplicity, natural materials, and asymmetry that exemplified the Wabi-Sabi aesthetic. This appreciation for imperfection and impermanence is also evident in the art of Kintsugi, where broken pottery is mended with gold, celebrating its history, and treasuring its flaws.

During a conversation with a Japanese friend, she recounted how Wabi-Sabi had significantly impacted her personal life, particularly in coping with stress stemming from the constant drive for perfection in today's high-pressure world. By incorporating Wabi-Sabi, she learned to find equilibrium, acknowledge her imperfections and those of others, and appreciate the transient moments of splendor and happiness life presents. In this light, Wabi-Sabi is more than an aesthetic philosophy; it represents a way of living that promotes mindfulness and wholehearted acceptance.

On the other hand, Kaizen is a philosophy deeply ingrained in the Japanese business world. As an outsider, I was initially surprised by the emphasis on continuous improvement, even in tasks that might appear trivial.

THE SIGNIFICANCE OF WABI-SABI, KAIZEN, AND IKIGAI IN JAPANESE CULTURE | 19

For example, I remember visiting a sushi restaurant where the itamae (sushi chef) had devoted years to mastering his art, driven by an innate passion for culinary artistry and a desire to provide guests with an unforgettable dining experience. This resolute dedication to perpetual progress clearly illustrates the Kaizen ethos.

Over time, I have come to understand that Kaizen extends far beyond the realm of business, influencing the lives of everyday Japanese people. From their morning rituals to their approach to education, the Japanese strive for self-improvement and growth in all aspects of life. This commitment to Kaizen has enabled Japan to become a global leader in innovation, efficiency, and quality.

Ikigai is a concept that resonates deeply within the hearts of the Japanese people, particularly in Okinawa, an island known for its high concentration of centenarians. During my time there, I was struck by the sense of purpose and joy that the elderly population exuded. Moreover, I had the privilege of listening to their inspiring stories that illustrated the integral role Ikigai played in their lives.

One centenarian, a sprightly gentleman, revealed his devotion to tending his vegetable garden. With great enthusiasm, he recounted how his daily ritual of nurturing the plants gave him a deep connection to nature. He experienced a sense of pride and satisfaction as he watched his garden thrive. Moreover, by sharing the fruits of his labor with his neighbors, he felt a tremendous sense of belonging within his community, which in turn nurtured his Ikigai.

Another elder, a spirited woman in her late nineties, shared her passion for pottery, a craft she had been perfecting for over seven decades. Her eyes shimmered as she described the joy of molding clay into functional works of art, expressing her creativity while contributing to her community. Her pottery brought people together and allowed her to share a piece of her soul with others, encapsulating her Ikigai.

A third elder, a lively woman in her early seventies, spoke of her love for traditional Okinawan dance. She had been dancing since her youth and continued to teach the younger generations, preserving the cultural heritage of her people. Her dedication to the art form and the bond it created among generations within her community filled her with a sense of purpose and fulfillment, embodying her Ikigai.

The heartwarming stories of passion, community connections, and devotion to their crafts from Okinawan elders exemplify the powerful impact of Ikigai on their lives, contributing to their sense of purpose, happiness, and longevity. However, I discovered that the concept of Ikigai transcends generational boundaries and serves as a guiding philosophy used by people of all ages.

At its core, Ikigai encourages individuals to search for purpose and significance in their daily lives by finding joy and fulfillment in their passions, relationships, and careers. It represents a holistic approach to life that values balance, harmony, and personal growth, deeply ingrained in the Japanese way of living. By adopting this philosophy, individuals can cultivate a greater sense of happiness and meaning in their lives, regardless of age or circumstance. Thus, the wisdom of Ikigai not only enriches the lives of Okinawan elders but serves as a beacon of inspiration for people from all walks of life.

Together, the concepts of Wabi-Sabi, Kaizen, and Ikigai, hold great significance in Japanese culture, shaping how people perceive beauty, approach self-improvement, and find purpose in their lives. These philosophies have left an indelible mark on Japan, and as we explore them further, we can begin to see how they might enrich our lives and perspectives.

CHAPTER 03

The Benefits of Adopting These Philosophies in Daily Life

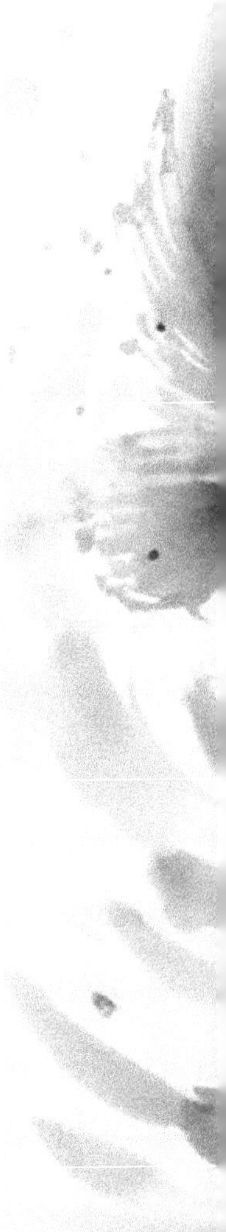

As I gaze out of my window, watching the delicate Sakura blossoms drifting gracefully to the ground, I cannot help but ponder on the transformative power that Wabi-Sabi, Kaizen, and Ikigai have had on my life. Over the past thirty years, I have not only studied these philosophies as a scholar, but I have also embraced them wholeheartedly, incorporating them into my daily routines and practices.

In this candid and personal chapter, I will share with you the ways in which adopting Wabi-Sabi, Kaizen, and Ikigai has transformed my life and how they can offer similar benefits to anyone willing to embrace their wisdom.

Wabi-Sabi: Appreciating Imperfection and Finding Beauty in Everyday Life

In an earlier phase of my life, I felt trapped in a cycle of monotony and self-doubt. My days were filled with seemingly endless routines, and I struggled to find meaning and satisfaction in my accomplishments. It was during this period of stagnation that I discovered Wabi-Sabi, which would ultimately catalyze a significant shift in my perspective and priorities.

Before my introduction to the philosophy of Wabi-Sabi, I was consumed with the pursuit of perfection, resulting in constant disappointment and frustration. However, as I began to appreciate the beauty in imperfection and transience, my outlook on life took a complete turn. Instead of focusing on what was lacking or imperfect, I began to see the unique character and beauty in flaws and irregularities. For instance, I now cherish the deep, almost black patina that covers my grandfather's once-yellow-gold pocket watch. This patina tells a story of the watch's age and history, which I find fascinating. My newfound appreciation for imperfection has allowed me to break free from the constraints of my perfectionist mindset, enabling me to find contentment in the fleeting nature of life.

By adopting Wabi-Sabi, I learned to see the extraordinary in the ordinary, to appreciate the beauty in the flaws, and to cherish each moment as a gift. This philosophy has opened my eyes to the wonders of the world and has given me a newfound sense of inner peace and contentment.

Kaizen: Continuous Improvement and Lifelong Learning

As a young entrepreneur, I was always looking for ways to improve efficiency and the bottom line. However, I often found myself overwhelmed by the enormity of the tasks at hand and struggled to prioritize my goals. It was not until I stumbled upon Kaizen that I realized the value of continuous improvement. By focusing on small, incremental changes, I was able to establish long-term, sustainable growth in both my business and personal life.

Kaizen has taught me the importance of patience and perseverance in achieving my goals. By analyzing and breaking down larger goals into smaller, more realistic steps, I have been able to build momentum and create a sense of progress, even during challenging times. In addition, this philosophy has encouraged me to become a lifelong learner, continually seeking new knowledge and experiences. Through Kaizen, I have cultivated a growth mindset, which has allowed me to face challenges with resilience and determination, ultimately leading to a more fulfilled and successful life.

Ikigai: Discovering Purpose and Cultivating Joy

Before encountering Ikigai, I often felt adrift, unsure of my place in the world or my reason for being. Sometimes I felt as though I merely existed without any real sense of fulfillment. However, as I began to search deeper into my passions, my strengths, and the ways in which I could contribute to the world, I uncovered a greater sense of purpose and meaning in my life.

Ikigai has demonstrated the vital importance of aligning my life with my core principles, enabling me to experience happiness and satisfaction in both work and personal endeavors. By discovering and nurturing my Ikigai, I have forged a deeper connection to my authentic self, resulting in an elevated sense of contentment.

Adopting the philosophies of Wabi-Sabi, Kaizen, and Ikigai in daily life has led to countless benefits, including inner peace, self-development, and motivation. As demonstrated through my personal experiences, these philosophies have the power to transform one's perspective and priorities, leading to a greater sense of contentment and fulfillment. As you embark on your own journey to embody these principles, I hope you, too, will experience the substantial transformation that comes with living a life guided by the wisdom of these ancient Japanese teachings.

Wabi-Sabi - The Beauty of Imperfection

CHAPTER 04

The origins and history of Wabi-Sabi

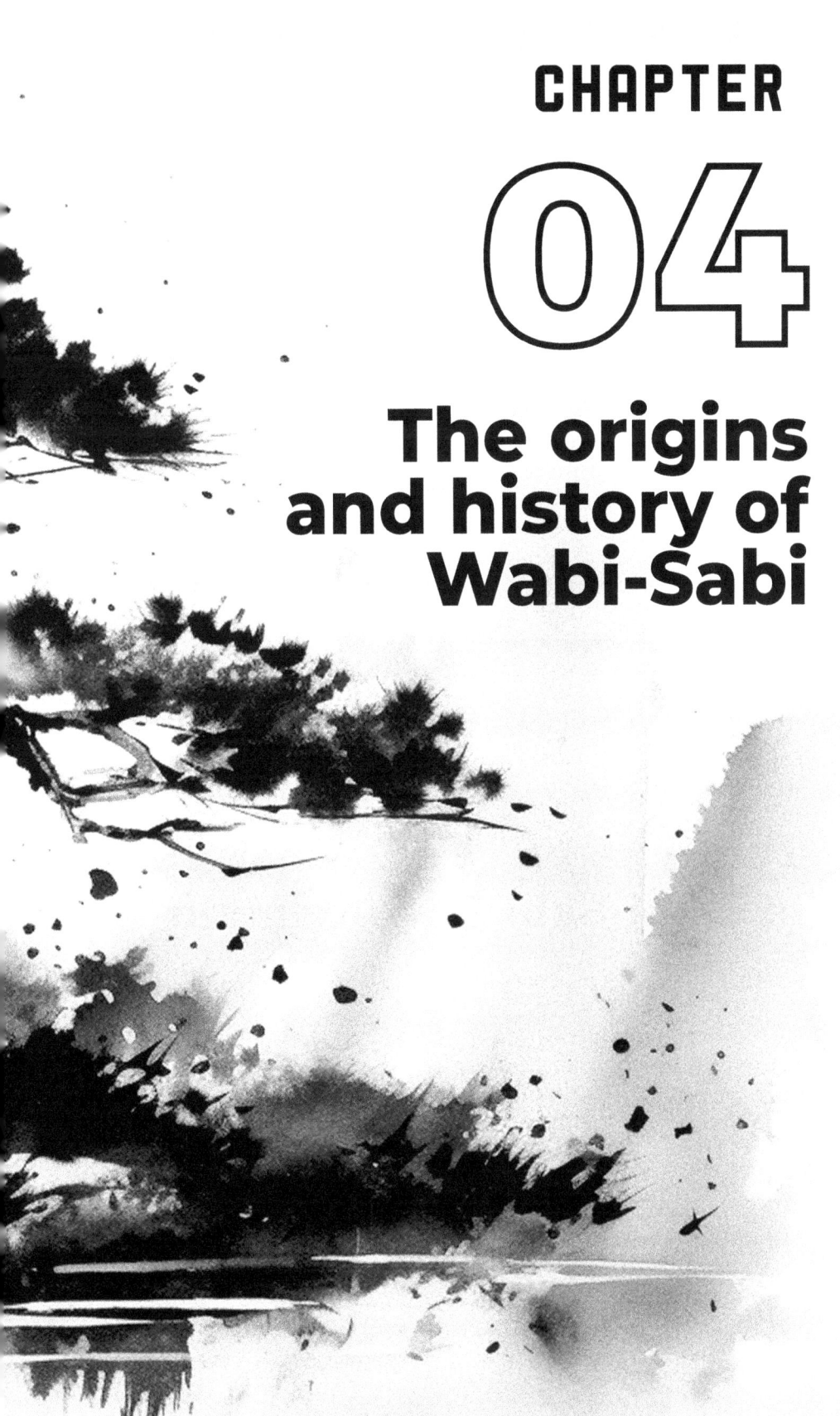

The Influence of Zen Buddhism

In the faintly lit meditation hall, the delicate aroma of sandalwood incense enveloping the room, I felt an intrinsic bond with the time-honored tradition of Zen Buddhism. During my studies in Japan, I came across the art of Koh-do, a traditional incense ceremony that opened my eyes to the deep relationship between Zen and the philosophy of Wabi-Sabi. At the heart of Zen lie teachings that underscore simplicity, mindfulness, and the value of the present moment, which have all significantly contributed to the development of Wabi-Sabi.

The roots of Wabi-Sabi can be traced back to the Zen teachings of impermanence, suffering, and the absence of self. In Zen, the recognition of these three characters of existence culminates in a deep comprehension of the true nature of reality, which in turn gives rise to the Wabi-Sabi aesthetic. The practice of Zen meditation, with its focus on direct experience and the cultivation of awareness, has played a vital role in forming the Wabi-Sabi mindset.

The Role of Tea Ceremonies in Wabi-Sabi Development

I still remember the first time I participated in a traditional Japanese tea ceremony, or "chanoyu," at a temple in Kyoto. As I knelt on the tatami mat, observing the deliberate and graceful movements of the tea master, I was struck by the deep sense of mindfulness and reverence that pervaded the ritual.

The tea ceremony, which has its origins in the Zen tradition, has been an integral part of developing Wabi-Sabi. The practice of chanoyu emphasizes the harmony between host and guest, the beauty of the natural materials used in the ceremony, and the fleeting nature of the experience itself. These elements have served as a fertile ground for the cultivation of the Wabi-Sabi aesthetic.

The tea master, Sen no Rikyu, who lived in the 16th century, is widely regarded as the father of the Wabi-Sabi tea ceremony. Rikyu sought to infuse the tea ceremony with the spirit of Zen, placing a strong emphasis on simplicity, rusticity, and the appreciation of imperfection. He favored humble tea utensils, often made from local materials, and designed tearooms with a sense of rustic beauty and harmony with nature.

Through Rikyu's influence, the principles of Wabi-Sabi began to permeate traditional tea ceremonies and, subsequently, the broader Japanese culture. As a result, the chanoyu became a powerful symbol of the Wabi-Sabi philosophy, a space in which participants could experience the subtle beauty of impermanence, imperfection, and incompleteness.

The origins and history of Wabi-Sabi are deeply entwined with the teachings of Zen Buddhism and the centuries-old practice of the tea ceremony. The influence of these two cultural forces has given rise to a unique aesthetic and philosophical outlook that reveres the beauty and fragility of life, emphasizing its ever-changing nature. As we continue to explore the world of Wabi-Sabi, we will delve deeper into the principles and practices that define this enigmatic and captivating philosophy.

CHAPTER 05

Core Principles of Wabi-Sabi

Imperfection

The first core principle of Wabi-Sabi is imperfection, or "Fukinsei" (不均整). This concept refers to the asymmetrical or irregular balance in a composition, where objects or elements are arranged in a way that is not perfectly symmetrical or evenly spaced. Wabi-Sabi encourages us to find value in imperfection, irregularity, and asymmetry in objects and art, finding beauty in the natural irregularities of the material or the hand of the maker.

I recall visiting a remote pottery workshop nestled in the mountains of Japan, where I observed the skilled artisans as they shaped and fired their clay creations. Each piece bore the marks of its maker—slight imperfections, irregularities, and unique characteristics that set it apart from any other. In the world of Wabi-Sabi, these imperfections are not only accepted but are revered, for they tell the story of the object's creation and reveal the human touch of the artist.

Incompleteness

The second core principle of Wabi-Sabi is incompleteness. Incompleteness can be beautiful and valuable, and it is embodied in the practice of Kintsugi, where the broken pieces of a damaged object are carefully reassembled using a special mix of gold, silver, or platinum lacquer. The result is a restored object that is both functional and beautiful, with the cracks and imperfections highlighted by the precious metal. Kintsugi is a powerful symbol of the transformative power of acceptance and self-love.

The concept of incompleteness is also evident in the Wabi-Sabi aesthetic of minimalism and simplicity, emphasizing negative space and allowing the observer's imagination to fill in the gaps. Through the practice of incompleteness, we can find contentment in the beauty of the unfinished and the evolving.

Impermanence

The third core principle of Wabi-Sabi is impermanence, or "mujō" (無常). This principle encapsulates the idea that all things are in constant change, and by recognizing and celebrating impermanence, we can appreciate the fleeting beauty of the world around us and cultivate a sense of gratitude for the present moment. A powerful example of impermanence can be seen in the delicate and short-lived beauty of cherry blossoms, known as "Sakura" in Japan. Every spring, these blossoms burst forth in a magnificent display of pink and white, only to fall from the trees a few weeks later, reminding us of the fleeting nature of life. By recognizing the impermanence of the cherry blossoms, we can appreciate their beauty all the more and cultivate a sense of gratitude for the present moment. Similarly, the Wabi-Sabi philosophy teaches us to find beauty and value in things that are impermanent, such as the changing seasons, the passage of time, and the natural decay of objects over time. By embracing impermanence, we can learn to cherish the beauty of the present moment and find contentment in the ever-changing nature of existence.

The core principles of Wabi-Sabi invite us to adopt a new outlook on beauty and the world around us. By integrating these principles into our daily lives, we can learn to cherish the fleeting and ever-changing nature of existence and appreciate the beauty in the imperfect, unfinished, and unconventional. Through the lens of Wabi-Sabi, we can find contentment in the beauty of the simple, the natural, and the authentic, and find harmony in the asymmetrical, irregular, and unpredictable.

CHAPTER 06

Wabi-Sabi Everyday in Art, Design, and Architecture

As I strolled along the quaint streets of Magome-juku, a well-preserved 17th-century Japanese village, I marveled at the effortless blending of Wabi-Sabi within the everyday existence of its inhabitants. From the weathered wooden facades of the houses to the asymmetrical arrangements of stones in the gardens, the beauty of imperfection was evident in every aspect of the art, design, and architecture around me. The Wabi-Sabi philosophy imbued a sense of calm and tranquility in the village, encouraging both locals and visitors to embrace the natural imperfections and appreciate the passage of time.

In the realm of art, Wabi-Sabi inspires spontaneity, freedom, and genuineness. The classic Japanese ink painting style, known as "Sumi-e" or "Suibokuga," is an excellent example of this ideology. Artists must learn to work with the unpredictability of the ink and the brush, embracing the imperfections and irregularities that emerge during the creative process. The resulting paintings possess a raw, unrefined beauty that resonates with the essence of Wabi-Sabi.

Within design, Wabi-Sabi manifests through the utilization of organic, unrefined materials and the honoring of handcrafted creations. A hand-carved wooden bowl, for example, may exhibit subtle variations in color, texture, and shape, each of which contributes to its exclusive character and allure. This respect for blemishes and individuality is also evident in the Japanese art of "Sashiko" (刺し子), characterized by a form of ornamental stitching often featuring uneven patterns and visible mending.

In architectural design, Wabi-Sabi is exemplified through the use of natural, locally sourced materials and a focus on simplicity, functionality, and harmony with the surrounding environment. Traditional Japanese homes, known as "Kominka" or simply "Minka," frequently feature exposed wooden beams, earthy plaster walls, and thatched roofs. The natural aging of these materials, with their cracks, discoloration, and weathering, only heightens their attractiveness and distinctive qualities.

One of the most iconic examples of Wabi-Sabi architecture is the Katsura Imperial Villa in Kyoto. The villa is marked by its subtle sophistication, the employment of humble materials, and a fluid layout that effortlessly blends with the adjacent landscape. The design features elements such as intentionally misaligned roof tiles and asymmetrical rooms, reflecting the Wabi-Sabi admiration for imperfection and natural charisma.

The tenets of Wabi-Sabi permeate numerous facets of daily life, spanning from art and design to architecture. By acknowledging imperfections and cherishing the handcrafted, natural, and distinct, we can infuse Wabi-Sabi wisdom into our existence and learn to recognize the concealed greatness in the world around us.

CHAPTER 07

Mindfulness and Acceptance of Life's Imperfections

EMBRACING IMPERFECTION

The gentle babbling streams and serene pathways of Kenrokuen Garden transported me to a state of inner peace. The garden, renowned for its natural beauty, embodies the essence of Wabi-Sabi in its subtle imperfections and appreciation for transience. With each step, I was reminded of the importance of accepting the world around me as it is, and to view flaws as an integral and valuable aspect of existence. It is a philosophy that is perfectly embodied in the delicate and ever-changing nature of Kenrokuen Garden. And so, as I sat beside the stream, feeling the cool breeze on my face and watching the sunlight slowly fade away, I was filled with a deep feeling of gratitude for the beauty that surrounds us all.

Mindfulness, a central tenet of both Wabi-Sabi and Zen Buddhism, involves being fully present and attentive to the current moment. By cultivating mindfulness, we can learn to value the simple beauty of our everyday experiences, from the delicate fragrance of a blooming flower to the soothing sound of raindrops on a windowpane. This practice enables us to see the world with fresh eyes, uncovering the hidden beauty that lies within life's imperfections. Through mindfulness, we can train ourselves to slow down and savor life's small pleasures rather than rushing from one moment to the next. In this way, we can find splendor and contentment in the ordinary and every day with a sense of gratitude and wonder.

One of the fundamental components of mindfulness is the practice of non-judgmental observation, which entails examining our thoughts, emotions, and experiences without categorizing them as good or bad. Through this practice, we can develop greater acceptance and compassion for ourselves and others, while recognizing that imperfection is an inherent part of the human experience. By integrating the Wabi-Sabi way of thinking into our mindfulness practice, we can learn to accept and even admire our own limitations, as well as those of others. This might involve exercising more patience with ourselves when we make mistakes or face setbacks, or extending kindness and understanding to a struggling friend or family member.

By integrating Wabi-Sabi into our mindfulness practice, we enhance our ability to navigate life's imperfections with grace and fortitude.

Additionally, practicing mindfulness and acceptance equips us to tackle life's challenges with increased resilience and composure. When dealing with hardships or disappointments, we can turn to the Wabi-Sabi doctrine of impermanence, recognizing that everything, both pleasant and unpleasant, is temporary and ever-changing. Adopting this outlook can instill a sense of inner peace and equilibrium, even during life's most challenging moments. The Wabi-Sabi philosophy offers precious lessons for developing mindfulness and embracing life's drawbacks. By valuing the beauty of impermanence and the inherent imperfection of the human experience, we can learn to live with increased compassion, resilience, and joy. Mindfulness grants us access to a deeper level of understanding, allowing us to find the remarkable within our everyday lives and uncover an abundance we might not have noticed otherwise.

CHAPTER 08

Incorporating Wabi-Sabi into Personal Growth

As I walked through the quiet, pictorial bamboo forest pathway at Hokokuji Temple, the whispering leaves and subtle swaying of the stalks emphasized the significance of personal growth and the ongoing quest for knowledge and adaptability. Nestled within the historic Kamakura district, this secluded temple, known as the "Bamboo Temple," offered a serene and contemplative atmosphere. It was during these moments that I felt a connection to the philosophy of Wabi-Sabi, which focuses on impermanence, imperfection, and incompleteness, presenting a novel lens through which to approach personal growth and self-improvement.

Embracing Imperfection and Vulnerability

Incorporating Wabi-Sabi into personal growth involves acknowledging our shortcomings and vulnerabilities. By recognizing that we all have inherent flaws, we can release ourselves from unrealistic expectations and self-judgment that hinder our progress. Accepting our imperfections does not mean that we should stop striving for improvement. Instead, it allows us to approach self-improvement from a place of self-compassion and humility, recognizing that we are all constantly evolving. This method helps us view setbacks and failures as opportunities for growth and enlightenment, rather than sources of embarrassment or disappointment.

Fostering Adaptability and Resilience

The Wabi-Sabi principle of impermanence reminds us that life undergoes constant transformation and that our ability to adapt and grow is essential for our well-being. A mindset of adaptability and resilience empowers us to approach life's uncertainties with curiosity and a sense of adventure, while maintaining a steadfast commitment to our values and priorities.

Developing elasticity involves cultivating a balanced perspective that acknowledges the transient nature of both successes and failures. When faced with difficulties or frustrations, we can draw on the wisdom of Wabi-Sabi to maintain a sense of serenity and trust in our ability to learn, grow, and persevere.

Pursuing Authenticity and Meaningful Connections

Wabi-Sabi provides a refreshing perspective on how we can approach our relationships and personal endeavors. It encourages us to embrace imperfection, which in turn leads to deeper and more authentic connections with others. When we recognize that everyone has flaws and that they are an inherent part of the human experience, we can let go of the pressure to be perfect and allow ourselves to be vulnerable with others. This vulnerability can help us create more robust and meaningful relationships, contributing to a sense of belonging, support, and fulfillment in our personal and professional lives.

Incorporating Wabi-Sabi into our personal growth journey involves staying true to our values and passions, rather than conforming to external expectations. By prioritizing what is truly meaningful, we can find a greater sense of purpose and satisfaction. This approach also allows us to develop a more compassionate and balanced approach to life, as we find new ways to navigate challenges and discover new paths.

Ultimately, the philosophy of Wabi-Sabi offers a roadmap for cultivating a more fulfilling and meaningful existence by embracing imperfection, vulnerability, authenticity, and adaptability. By following this course, we can create deeper connections, find greater fulfillment, and live more fully in the present moment.

PART 2

Kaizen - The Art of Continuous Improvement

CHAPTER 09

The Origins and History of Kaizen

The streets of Tokyo were a feast for the senses, with vibrant colors, tantalizing smells, and a constant buzz of activity. Marveling at the cutting-edge technology and architecture around me, I could not help but feel a sense of awe at the Japanese commitment to excellence. This dedication to constant improvement and innovation is the heart of Kaizen, a philosophy ingrained in Japanese culture for centuries and has since spread worldwide, inspiring countless individuals and industries.

Early Beginnings

The word Kaizen (改善) is derived from two Japanese characters: "kai" (改), meaning "change," and "zen" (善), meaning "good" or "better." The concept of continuous improvement has been an integral part of Japanese culture for centuries, originating from the country's intrinsic values of harmony, balance, and a strong work ethic. One of the earliest examples of Kaizen can be traced back to the Edo period (1603 – 1868), during which Japan experienced a period of relative peace and stability. During this time, various craftsmen and artisans sought to perfect their skills and techniques, driven by a deep-seated belief in the pursuit of excellence and mastery.

Influence of the Toyota Production System

The modern concept of Kaizen, as it is known today, was largely shaped by the Toyota Production System (TPS), a management philosophy that emerged in post-World War II Japan. Under the leadership of Taiichi Ohno, Toyota sought to develop an innovative approach to production that would enable the company to compete with established Western automobile manufacturers. Central to the TPS was the idea of continuous improvement, or Kaizen, which encouraged workers at all levels of the organization to seek and implement small, incremental improvements in processes, procedures, and overall efficiency. This focus on continuous improvement not only allowed Toyota to dramatically increase its productivity and quality, but also led to the development of innovative production techniques, such as just-in-time manufacturing and the use of kanban cards.

The Global Spread of Kaizen

The success of the Toyota Production System and its focus on continuous improvement quickly caught the attention of businesses and industries around the world. In the 1980s, the concept of Kaizen began to gain widespread recognition as organizations sought to emulate Toyota's innovative approach to production and management. Today, the principles of Kaizen have been adopted by companies in various industries worldwide, from manufacturing and healthcare to education and technology. By implementing the concept of continuous improvement, organizations, and individuals alike can foster a culture of innovation, adaptability, and excellence, ultimately leading to greater success and fulfillment.

In summary, the history and development of Kaizen demonstrate the importance of continuous improvement and innovation in achieving excellence. The philosophy has been ingrained in Japanese culture for centuries and was further developed through the Toyota Production System, leading to significant improvements in productivity and quality. The global spread of Kaizen has enabled organizations across various industries to foster a culture of innovation and adaptability, ultimately leading to greater success and fulfillment. The philosophy of Kaizen reminds us that there is always room for improvement, and that continuous efforts to refine and perfect our work can lead to greatness.

CHAPTER 10

The Post-World War II Japanese Economic Miracle

As I stood atop the observation deck of the Tokyo Skytree, a modern architectural marvel, and the world's tallest freestanding broadcasting tower, I took in the panoramic view of the sprawling metropolis below. With its completion in 2012, the Tokyo Skytree has become an emblematic representation of the city's perseverance and innovation. I was awed by the extraordinary transformation Japan had undergone in the decades following World War II. From the ashes of war, the country had risen to become an economic powerhouse driven by innovation, hard work, and a steadfast commitment to the principles of Kaizen.

Reconstruction and the Role of Government

In the aftermath of World War II, Japan faced the daunting task of rebuilding its devastated economy and infrastructure. The government played a crucial role in this process, implementing a series of comprehensive economic policies and initiatives tailored to catalyze rapid industrial growth and development. Among these initiatives was the establishment of the Ministry of International Trade and Industry (MITI) (now known as the Ministry of Economy, Trade and Industry (METI)). It played a central role in coordinating and supporting the expansion of Japan's key industries, and the introduction of a series of "Five-Year Economic Plans," which set ambitious growth targets for various sectors of the economy.

The Role of Kaizen in Japan's Economic Success

At the heart of Japan's post-war economic miracle was the adoption and widespread implementation of the principles of Kaizen. As Japanese companies and industries practiced the concept of continuous improvement, they were able to achieve exceptional levels of efficiency, productivity, and innovation. One of the principal factors that contributed to the success of Kaizen in Japan was the emphasis on employee involvement and empowerment. By encouraging workers at all levels of the organization to identify and implement improvements, Japanese companies could tap into a wealth of creativity and expertise, driving continued growth and development. Furthermore, the principles of Kaizen nurtured a culture of collaboration and teamwork within Japanese organizations, as employees worked together to solve problems and overcome challenges. This collaborative approach played a vital role in developing groundbreaking technologies and products, which helped propel Japan to the forefront of the global economy.

The Influence of Japan's Economic Miracle on the World

The astonishing success of the Japanese economy during the post-war period had a groundbreaking impact on the global economic landscape. As Japanese companies gained prominence and market share in key sectors such as automobiles, electronics, and consumer goods, they not only transformed their own nation's economy, but also inspired and influenced other countries across the world. The success of companies such as Toyota, Sony, and Panasonic, which were built on the principles of Kaizen, led to the widespread adoption of these principles in industries across the globe. Moreover, as businesses worldwide sought to replicate Japan's economic success, they began to realize the value of employee empowerment, collaboration, and continuous improvement.

The influence of Japan's economic miracle also extended to the realm of international trade. The country's emphasis on export-oriented growth strategies helped it become one of the world's largest exporters of goods and services, and its trade surplus with the United States and other countries sparked international debate over trade imbalances and protectionism.

Today, Japan's economic landscape has evolved, and the country faces new challenges, such as an aging population and increasing competition from other nations. However, the principles of Kaizen and continuous improvement remain a core component of Japan's business culture and continue to drive innovation and growth in various industries. The legacy of Japan's post-war economic miracle is a testament to the transformative power of visionary economic policies, hard work, and a steadfast commitment to excellence.

CHAPTER 11

The Role of Kaizen in Japanese Industries

As I toured the halls of a state-of-the-art Japanese confectionery factory, renowned for producing some of the nation's most beloved snacks, I was spellbound by the flawless melding of innovative technology and human know-how. The secret to this symbiotic union was the pervasive philosophy of Kaizen, which has been instrumental in the success of numerous Japanese industries.

Manufacturing and Automotive Industry

Kaizen principles have revolutionized the way that Japanese manufacturing and automotive companies operate. Companies such as Toyota, Honda, and Nissan have achieved unparalleled success in terms of efficiency, productivity, and excellence across their product lines, thanks to their continuous improvement methodologies. Furthermore, this remarkable progress was only possible due to a culture that empowered employees at all levels within an organization—creating opportunities for innovation and collaboration. Consequently, these successful Japanese manufacturers developed methods such as lean manufacturing, just-in-time production, and total quality management. These techniques are now recognized worldwide as essential components of modern operation processes.

Electronics and Technology Industry

Japan's electronics and technology industries have taken the concept of Kaizen to heart, driving their relentless pursuit for improvement. Major players such as Sony, Panasonic, and Toshiba have harnessed their continuous improvement methodology to drive innovation in different processes, from streamlining operations for greater efficiency to eliminating wasteful practices that only consume resources without any tangible benefit.

This collective problem-solving approach championed by Kaizen continues to be a cornerstone of Japanese electronic companies' pursuit of excellence, making them industry leaders in product design, development, and delivery on an international scale.

Service Industries

The influence of Kaizen extends beyond the manufacturing and technology sectors, reaching into various service industries such as retail, hospitality, and healthcare. For example, companies like Uniqlo, a Japanese trendsetting fashion industry leader, have incorporated Kaizen principles to optimize their supply chain, inventory management, and customer service. Meanwhile, in the hospitality industry, renowned Japanese hotels and Ryokans have employed Kaizen to enhance guest experiences, streamline operations, and maintain the highest service standards. Similarly, Japanese hospitals and clinics have adopted Kaizen methodologies in the healthcare sector to improve patient care, reduce waiting times, and optimize resource allocation.

Small and Medium-Sized Enterprises (SMEs)

The fundamentals of Kaizen have proven to be an invaluable tool for success in Japan for small and medium-sized enterprises (SMEs) across Japan. This approach bolsters competitiveness and encourages adaptability through innovation throughout the business landscape—a quality essential for global sustainability. Furthermore, this acclaimed technique of continuous improvement drives creative solutions that can better equip companies with improved competitiveness and enhanced productivity while cultivating an adaptive atmosphere of excellence. In this way, Kaizen standards have empowered many industries, from manufacturing to services across Japan—and beyond—to stay ahead amidst a fierce global marketplace.

In summary, the pervasive influence of Kaizen on Japanese industries has been a remarkable success story that continues to inspire companies worldwide. From manufacturing and automotive to electronics and technology, service industries, and small and medium-sized enterprises, Kaizen has proven to be a powerful tool for driving innovation, excellence, and sustainability.

By empowering employees at all levels to identify and implement improvements, Japanese companies have created a culture of continuous improvement and collaboration, promoting growth and development across diverse sectors of the economy. The value of Kaizen as a catalyst of success in Japanese industries cannot be overstated, and its principles provide a valuable guide for companies worldwide seeking to remain competitive in an ever-changing global marketplace.

CHAPTER 12

Core Principles of Kaizen

While I wandered through the Omiya Bonsai Village, home to a remarkable collection of exquisite bonsai trees representing centuries of cultivation and dedication, I had an illuminating epiphany. The same principles that govern the art of bonsai also underlie the essence of Kaizen. By adhering to its fundamental tenets—continuous improvement and growth—organizations and individuals alike can achieve enduring success and reach unprecedented heights in their pursuit of excellence.

Incremental Improvement

At the core of Kaizen is the belief that small, incremental improvements can lead to significant and sustainable results over time. By focusing on gradual, ongoing enhancements to processes and systems, institutions can achieve continuous growth and development without the need for large-scale, disruptive changes. This principle encourages organizations and individuals to view improvement as an ongoing journey rather than a destination to be reached. By employing the mindset of constant progress, we can cultivate a more adaptive and resilient approach to change, ultimately leading to enhanced levels of success and fulfillment.

Employee Involvement

Kaizen emphasizes the importance of involving employees at all levels within the company in the process of identifying and implementing improvements. By encouraging input and ideas from every team member, organizations can tap into a wealth of creativity, expertise, and diverse perspectives, resulting in more effective and innovative solutions. In addition to promoting innovation, employee involvement in the Kaizen process encourages a sense of accountability and responsibility as individuals become increasingly invested in achieving organizational goals. This can lead to increased motivation, engagement, job satisfaction, and higher morale among team members.

Waste Elimination

One of the core principles of Kaizen is the focus on eliminating waste, or "muda" (無駄), in all its forms. Waste can take many shapes, such as excess inventory, unnecessary motion, or defects in products or processes. By identifying and eliminating sources of waste, organizations can streamline their operations, reduce costs, and increase efficiency. Waste elimination in Kaizen goes beyond merely eradicating physical waste. This ethos also encompasses addressing wasted time, limited resources, and efforts that do not add value to the end product or service. By targeting waste, organizations can create a leaner and more efficient operation that is better equipped to meet the needs of clients and stakeholders.

Standardization

Standardization is a critical principle in the Kaizen philosophy, as it provides a foundation for measuring and comparing performance. By establishing standardized processes and procedures, organizations can ensure consistent quality, reduce variability, and create a baseline for identifying areas of improvement. In addition, by setting standards across different teams and departments, organizations can facilitate knowledge sharing that leads to learning from successes as well as failures—driving the continuous process of improving performance.

To sum up, the principles of Kaizen have been time-tested and proven to drive growth and development. The emphasis on incremental improvement encourages a steady and sustainable pace of progress, while employee involvement cultivates a sense of ownership and responsibility for the success of the organization. In addition, waste elimination and standardization further streamline operations and ensure consistent quality, all while promoting a culture of efficiency and innovation. By embracing these principles, organizations and individuals can create a pathway toward lasting success and fulfillment, fueled by the pursuit of excellence and continuous improvement.

CHAPTER 13

The PDCA Cycle and the 5S Methodology

The PDCA Cycle (Plan-Do-Check-Act)

During my trip to a renowned Japanese auto factory, I was struck by the level of diligence and precision that was evident in every aspect of the operation. It was clear that every step of the manufacturing process had been carefully planned and meticulously executed, with a keen focus on maximizing efficiency and minimizing waste. Moreover, as I observed the workers, I realized that they were constantly engaged in a continuous methodology of improvement, utilizing the PDCA (Plan, Do, Check, Act) cycle to identify areas for optimization and make iterative changes to their processes. This is the cornerstone of Kaizen.

The PDCA cycle is a four-step iterative process designed to promote continuous improvement by encouraging a structured approach to problem-solving and decision-making. The PDCA cycle is broken down to:

01 Plan

Identify a problem or area of improvement and develop a plan to address it. This involves gathering data, analyzing the current situation, and setting specific goals and targets.

02 Do

Implement the plan on a small scale, testing the proposed changes to observe their effects and gather data for analysis.

03 Check
Evaluate the results of the implemented changes, comparing the outcomes to the original goals and targets. Analyze the data to determine the effectiveness of the plan and identify any areas for further improvement.

04 Act
If the plan has proven to be effective, implement the changes on a larger scale and standardize the new process. If additional refinements are needed, revise the plan, and repeat the cycle.

By following the PDCA cycle, organizations can cultivate a culture of continuous learning and improvement, ensuring that they remain adaptable and responsive to the changing needs of their customers and the market.

The 5S Methodology (Sort, Set in Order, Shine, Standardize, Sustain)

As I toured the immaculate factory, I quickly noticed the pristine order and tidiness that pervaded the workspace. This, I discovered, was the result of the 5S methodology, another key element of Kaizen philosophy. The 5S method is an orderly approach to workplace organization and efficiency designed to create a clean, organized, and safe work environment that promotes productivity and reduces waste.

The five steps of the 5S methodology are:

01 Sort (Seiri)

Remove unnecessary items from the workspace and only keep what is essential for the tasks being performed. This helps minimize clutter and distractions, making focusing on the work at hand easier.

02 Set in Order (Seiton)

Organize the workspace in a logical, efficient manner, ensuring that tools, materials, and resources are easily accessible and stored in designated locations. This helps to streamline workflow and reduce wasted time searching for items.

03 Shine (Seiso)

Regularly clean and maintain the workspace, ensuring that equipment and tools are in good working order and the environment is free from dirt, debris, and potential hazards. This promotes a sense of pride and ownership in the workspace and helps to prevent accidents and equipment breakdowns.

04 Standardize (Seiketsu)

Develop standardized processes and procedures for maintaining the first three S's, ensuring that workplace organization and cleanliness are consistently maintained.

05 Sustain (Shitsuke)

Foster a culture of continuous improvement and commitment to the 5S methodology, ensuring employees are engaged and actively involved in maintaining an organized, efficient workspace.

In conclusion, the PDCA cycle and the 5S methodology are two essential components of the Kaizen philosophy, revolutionizing how organizations approach problem-solving and continuous improvement. By following the structured approach of the PDCA cycle, organizations can identify areas for optimization, test proposed changes, evaluate their effectiveness, and implement them on a larger scale to standardize new processes. Similarly, by implementing the 5S methodology, organizations can create a work environment that promotes efficiency, productivity, and safety. Both methods emphasize the importance of continuous learning and improvement, supporting the overall goals of the Kaizen philosophy. By utilizing these tools, organizations can cultivate a culture of excellence and innovation, ensuring that they remain adaptable and responsive to the changing needs of their customers and the market.

CHAPTER 14
Kaizen in Everyday Life

Applying Kaizen in Personal Development

As I stood at Jodogahama Beach, mesmerized by the stunning juxtaposition of serene blue waters and the imposing, jagged white rocks that lined the shore, I found myself in a moment of deep contemplation. Surrounded by this breathtaking landscape, I pondered the myriad ways we could incorporate Kaizen principles into our daily lives, especially considering how this philosophy of continuous improvement could become a potent catalyst for personal development and self-enhancement. And just as the natural beauty of Jodogahama Beach is the result of constant erosion and shaping by the elements, so too can we shape ourselves through the ongoing process of Kaizen.

Setting Small, Achievable Goals

One of the key components of Kaizen is the focus on incremental improvement, which can be highly effective when applied to personal development. By setting small, achievable goals, we can make steady progress toward our larger objectives, building confidence and momentum along the way. For example, if you wish to improve your physical fitness, you might start by committing to a daily 10-minute walk. Over time, you could gradually increase the duration and intensity of your walks, eventually incorporating more strenuous exercises into your routine.

Cultivating Mindfulness and Self-Awareness

Kaizen also emphasizes the importance of reflection and self-awareness as part of the improvement process. By regularly evaluating our thoughts, actions, and habits, we can identify areas for improvement and develop strategies to address them.

In addition, practicing mindfulness and meditation can aid the process by providing a heightened awareness of thoughts, emotions, and behaviors that may impede progress or mask strengths, so they remain untapped. By becoming more aware internally, we are better positioned to achieve real growth on both personal and professional levels.

Embracing Lifelong Learning

The principle of continuous improvement encourages us to view personal development as an ongoing journey rather than a destination to be reached. By adopting a mindset of lifelong learning, we can remain open to new experiences, ideas, and perspectives, continually expanding our knowledge and skill set. To embrace lifelong learning, consider seeking new learning opportunities, such as taking classes, attending workshops, or joining clubs and organizations related to your interests. Additionally, make a habit of reading, listening to podcasts, or watching documentaries on a wide range of topics, as this can help to expand your perspective and enrich your understanding of the world.

Applying the PDCA Cycle and the 5S Methodology

The PDCA cycle and the 5S methodology can also be applied to personal development, providing a well-structured framework for pinpointing areas of improvement, and facilitating changes. By adhering to the steps of the PDCA cycle, you can design, and test new strategies tailored to personal growth. Concurrently, the 5S methodology can help you create an organized, efficient, and supportive environment that promotes productivity and well-being.

To summarize, by applying the principles of Kaizen to our everyday lives, we can foster a mindset of perpetual growth and self-improvement. As a result, we can experience increased fulfillment, success, and happiness as we continuously strive to become the best versions of ourselves.

CHAPTER 15

Implementing Kaizen in Work and Professional Growth

Implementing Kaizen in Work and Professional Growth

As I entered the small workshop, the clacking of the loom greeted me. Here, I was privileged to observe an award-winning master textile weaver at work. Her nimble fingers moved in a precise dance, creating intricate patterns and designs on the fabric. The weaver's passion for her artisanship was contagious, and it was evident that she had found fulfillment and purpose in her work. As I watched her meticulous attention to detail and unwavering focus, I thought about how Kaizen could be applied to our professional lives.

By exercising a mindset of continuous improvement, we can strive to perfect our craft and achieve more success in our careers. Just as the weaver sought to perfect even the most minor details in her work, we too can hone our skills and expertise, and consistently seek to better ourselves. Pursuing excellence can open new opportunities for growth and advancement in our professions, ultimately leading to greater fulfillment and satisfaction.

Pursuing Mastery through Deliberate Practice

One of the core aspects of Kaizen is the focus on incremental improvement, which can be achieved through deliberate practice. By continually refining our skills and pushing ourselves to reach new levels of proficiency, we can attain mastery in our chosen field. To engage in deliberate practice, identify specific areas of your work that you wish to improve and set targeted goals for your development. Then, create a plan to work on these areas consistently, dedicating time and effort to hone your skills through repetition, feedback, and reflection.

Embrace a Growth Mindset

Having a mindset that prioritizes growth is essential for incorporating Kaizen into our careers. When we believe our skills and abilities can be developed through hard work and dedication, we are more likely to approach obstacles with an open mind and a willingness to learn from our mistakes. To cultivate a growth-oriented mindset, it is imperative to view setbacks and downfalls as opportunities for growth rather than insurmountable obstacles. Additionally, it is crucial to welcome feedback from colleagues and supervisors as a valuable tool for identifying areas for improvement and guiding ongoing development.

Fostering Collaboration and Teamwork

The principle of employee involvement in Kaizen encourages collaboration and teamwork, which can be powerful drivers of professional growth. You can foster an environment that promotes continuous learning and improvement by actively engaging with your colleagues, sharing knowledge and best practices, and working together to solve problems. To encourage collaboration and teamwork, take the initiative to reach out to your colleagues, offering your support and expertise when needed. Participate in team meetings and brainstorming sessions, actively contributing your ideas and perspectives to help drive innovation and progress.

Applying the PDCA Cycle and the 5S Methodology in the Workplace

The PDCA cycle and the 5S methodology can also be utilized to support professional growth, providing a structured approach to identifying and implementing improvements in the workplace. Applying the PDCA cycle to your work processes allows you to develop and assess new strategies for enhancing your performance and productivity.

The 5S methodology can help create an organized, efficient, and effective work environment supporting your professional development. By implementing the 5S principles in your workspace, you can minimize distractions, streamline your workflow, and create a more favorable environment for learning and progress.

In summary, incorporating the principles of Kaizen into our professional lives can lead to a multitude of benefits. By consistently seeking to improve ourselves and our work, we can refine our skills, boost our performance, and open new doors of opportunity for advancement. In doing so, we can reach our full potential and contribute to the success and prosperity of our organizations and the wider community. The continuous pursuit of excellence, inspired by Kaizen, can drive innovation, improve efficiency, and increase overall satisfaction and fulfillment in our work. Additionally, as we become more adept at implementing Kaizen, we can serve as role models and advocates for a culture of continuous improvement, positively impacting the lives and careers of those around us.

CHAPTER 16

Kaizen in Relationships and Communication

During my visit to Kinkaku-ji, a Zen Buddhist temple, I was captivated by the tranquil scenery of the temple grounds. The shimmering reflection of the golden pavilion on the pond, the carefully manicured gardens, and the surrounding forest all seemed to coexist in perfect harmony. As I absorbed the setting, I realized that this balance and harmony could serve as a model for our interactions with others. By applying the principles of Kaizen to our relationships and communication, we can create deeper connections and improve our emotional intelligence, leading to more fulfilling and satisfying interactions with those around us.

Cultivating Active Listening Skills

To apply the principles of Kaizen to relationships and communication, one primary aspect is focusing on continuous improvement, which can be done by enhancing our listening skills. By becoming better listeners, we can understand others' perspectives, demonstrate empathy, and create stronger bonds. For example, in the workplace, a manager could improve relationships with their team by using active listening to listen to their concerns, ideas, and suggestions, and in doing so, demonstrate respect for their team members and create a more collaborative and productive work environment. To practice active listening, one must give their full attention to the speaker, avoid distractions, and resist the urge to interrupt. By taking time to reflect on the message and asking questions to ensure complete understanding, a foundation for open and honest communication is created. This approach not only shows respect for the speaker but also fosters deeper relationships built on trust, respect, and understanding.

Developing Emotional Intelligence

By developing emotional intelligence, we can improve our ability to navigate complex social situations, express ourselves more effectively, and forge stronger connections in our relationships and communication. For instance, in a family setting, practicing Kaizen can help foster stronger relationships between family members by encouraging open communication, active listening, and respect for one another's perspectives. Family members can work together to identify areas for improvement, offer constructive feedback, and support one another in achieving shared goals. To enhance emotional intelligence, we can practice self-awareness by reflecting on our feelings and their impact on our behavior. We can develop empathy by putting ourselves in others' shoes, trying to understand their sentiments and perspectives, and strengthening emotional regulation by learning to recognize and manage our emotional triggers and reactions.

Nurturing Open and Honest Communication

Incorporating the principles of Kaizen can lead to candid and transparent dialogue, which is vital for identifying areas needing improvement and stimulating collaboration. By prioritizing openness and sincerity in our interactions with others, we can establish an environment of trust, respect, and mutual understanding. For instance, in a community setting, members can utilize Kaizen to encourage open and honest communication for the benefit of the community. By working together and exchanging ideas, the organization can identify areas for growth and implement changes that better serve the community's needs. To foster an atmosphere of honesty and openness, it is essential to express your thoughts and emotions freely, while also being receptive to the perspectives of others. Promoting dialogue by asking questions and inviting feedback helps create a collaborative environment that facilitates the exchange of ideas and opinions.

Applying the PDCA Cycle to Relationship Building

By integrating the principles of Kaizen into our interpersonal connections through the PDCA cycle, we can determine and improve areas requiring development, leading to more meaningful and fulfilling relationships. For instance, in a romantic relationship setting, a couple seeking to enhance their communication and relationship could use the PDCA cycle as an adaptable framework. They could set a goal of having more meaningful conversations and apply the PDCA cycle's distinct stages by planning out a discussion topic, actively engaging in the conversation, checking in on each other's emotions and reactions, and adjusting their communication strategy as necessary. In doing so, they can continually refine their interpersonal skills and deepen their connection with one another.

As we strive for continuous improvement, we not only enrich our lives, but also contribute to the well-being and happiness of our loved ones and the broader community. Real-life examples of how Kaizen has been applied to relationships and communication in different contexts, such as in the workplace, family, or community settings, demonstrate the practical benefits of this philosophy in improving our relationships and interactions. By embracing Kaizen in our everyday lives, we can create more meaningful and fulfilling connections with those around us.

Ikigai - The Reason for Being

CHAPTER 17

The Origins and History of Ikigai

The Origins and History of Ikigai

Surrounded by the picturesque Shukkei-en Garden, I stood mesmerized by the vivid colors of the koi fish that seemed to dance in the pond. The graceful movements of the majestic koi prompted me to think about Ikigai, a Japanese philosophy that aims to reveal our "reason for being." Rooted in centuries of tradition and wisdom, Ikigai encourages us to find our true purpose in life and live in harmony with ourselves and the world around us.

Ancient Roots

The concept of Ikigai can be traced back to ancient Japanese culture and spiritual beliefs. In particular, the term "iki" (生き), which means "life," and "gai" (甲斐), which represents "value" or "worth," encapsulate the idea of finding joy, purpose, and meaning in our existence. While the precise origins of Ikigai are difficult to pinpoint, its core principles can be found in various aspects of Japanese history, art, and spirituality.

The Influence of Buddhism and Shintoism

Both Buddhism and Shintoism, two of the most prominent religious traditions in Japan, have played a significant role in shaping the concept of Ikigai. Buddhism, with its emphasis on mindfulness, compassion, and the pursuit of enlightenment, has inspired many of the ideas that underlie Ikigai, including the importance of finding inner harmony and living in the present moment. Shintoism, Japan's Indigenous religion, also contributes to the philosophy of Ikigai through its focus on the interconnectedness of all things and the divine nature of life itself. By recognizing the sacredness of our existence and the interconnected web of relationships that bind us to the world, Shintoism encourages us to find meaning and purpose in our daily lives.

The Role of Samurai and Bushido

The samurai, Japan's famed warrior class, and their code of Bushido have also played a part in shaping the concept of Ikigai. Bushido, also known as "the way of the warrior," is a set of moral principles and guidelines that govern the behavior of the samurai. These principles, which include honor, loyalty, and self-discipline, emphasize the importance of living a life of purpose, duty, and integrity. By adhering to the tenets of Bushido, the samurai were expected to find their Ikigai in their dedication to their lord and their commitment to protecting their people. Pursuing Ikigai, for the samurai, was a lifelong journey that required unwavering focus, discipline, and self-reflection.

Modern-Day Ikigai in Japanese Culture

The principles of Ikigai have been integrated into Japanese culture in numerous ways, from traditional arts to modern business methods. For example, the tea ceremony, or "Chanoyu," is an example of how Ikigai has influenced Japanese culture. The practice of Chanoyu involves preparing and presenting tea to guests in a highly ritualized manner, with an emphasis on mindfulness, harmony, and respect. The process of preparing and serving the tea is a meditative practice that aims to bring participants into the present moment and foster a sense of tranquility and connection.

In addition to the tea ceremony, pottery, or "Yakimono" (焼き物), is another example of how Ikigai has influenced Japanese culture. Pottery making involves a deep connection to the natural world and requires a focus on mindfulness, patience, and self-reflection. By engaging in pottery making, individuals can find their Ikigai in the creation process and the connection to the natural world.

Moreover, in modern business practices, Ikigai has been incorporated into the concept of "Hatarakigai" (働きがい), which translates to "work worth doing." The idea is that individuals can find greater satisfaction and fulfillment in their work when they see it as a meaningful and purposeful endeavor. This can lead to increased motivation, productivity, and overall job satisfaction. By exploring the various ways in which Ikigai has been applied throughout Japanese history and culture, the author can provide readers with a deeper understanding of the philosophy and its practical applications.

In conclusion, Ikigai is a timeless philosophy that has guided Japanese culture for centuries, permeating everything from art and spirituality to modern business practices. We can live a more purposeful and satisfying life by embracing the fundamental principles of finding meaning, joy, and purpose through our passions, values, and talents. Whether through the ritualized practice of Chanoyu, the meditative art of pottery making, or finding fulfillment in our work through Hatarakigai, Ikigai offers practical tools for self-discovery and growth. By following this philosophy, we can broaden our understanding of ourselves and the world around us, leading to enhanced fulfillment, happiness, and inner tranquility. With its wisdom drawn from ancient customs and past generations, Ikigai is a robust framework that can inspire us to find our reason for being and live in harmony with ourselves and the world.

CHAPTER 18

The Concept of Ikigai in Okinawan Culture

Okinawa, an archipelago located in southern Japan, is renowned for its vibrant culture, unique traditions, and, most notably, its extraordinary longevity. While wandering the scenic coastlines of this idyllic island, I pondered the significance of Ikigai within Okinawan culture and its potential influence on the exceptional health and well-being of the local population.

Longevity and the "Blue Zones"

Okinawa is often referred to as one of the world's "Blue Zones," a term coined by researchers to describe regions where people live significantly longer, healthier lives than the global average. The exceptional longevity of the Okinawan people has been attributed to numerous factors, including a healthy diet high in plant-based foods and low in meat and dairy products, as well as the practice of Hara Hachi Bu, a tradition of eating until one is only 80% full that promotes a healthy balance of caloric intake. Regular physical activity, such as gardening, walking, and other forms of low-impact exercise, is also a common practice in Okinawa and is believed to contribute to the region's longevity. Furthermore, the importance of social connections in Okinawan culture extends beyond Moai, as Okinawans also highly value intergenerational relationships and respect for elders. However, researchers have also identified the importance of Ikigai in Okinawan culture, suggesting that pursuing one's purpose in life may play a crucial role in promoting wellness.

Ikigai in Okinawan Daily Life

In Okinawan culture, the concept of Ikigai is deeply woven into the fabric of daily life. From an early age, Okinawans are encouraged to discover their Ikigai and to pursue their passions, talents, and interests with fervor and dedication. This pursuit of one's purpose is not limited to professional accomplishments but also extends to personal relationships, community involvement, and spiritual growth. Many Okinawans believe their Ikigai is closely tied to their sense of identity and their place within the community, which, in turn, helps to create strong social bonds and support networks that contribute to their overall well-being and happiness. In addition to strong social connections, regular physical activity is also a common practice in Okinawa and is believed to contribute to the region's longevity.

Therefore, many Okinawans incorporate low to moderate-intensity forms of exercise to stay active and healthy. By cultivating a sense of purpose through Ikigai and prioritizing physical activity, Okinawans have created a unique and inspiring blueprint for living a long, healthy, and fulfilling life.

The Role of Moai

One of the most distinctive aspects of Okinawan culture is the tradition of "moai" (模合), or social support groups. These close-knit groups of friends, neighbors, and family members provide mutual assistance and emotional support, reinforcing the importance of community and social connections in attaining Ikigai. Moai members typically share similar values, interests, and life goals, and they come together to celebrate achievements, offer encouragement, and provide a sense of belonging. The importance of social connections in Okinawan culture extends beyond Moai, as Okinawans also place a high value on intergenerational relationships and respect for elders. By participating in Moai and fostering these intergenerational relationships, Okinawans cultivate a strong sense of community and purpose, which contributes to their overall well-being and longevity. The concept of Ikigai is an integral component of Okinawan culture, providing individuals with a sense of purpose and direction in life. By emphasizing the importance of finding one's purpose and nurturing strong social connections, the people of Okinawa have created a unique and inspiring blueprint for living a long, healthy, and fulfilling life.

In conclusion, the concept of Ikigai is a fundamental component of Okinawan culture and a key factor in the region's exceptional longevity and well-being. Through nurturing strong social connections and pursuing one's purpose in life, the people of Okinawa have created a unique and inspiring blueprint for living a fulfilling and meaningful life. By incorporating the principles of Ikigai into our own lives, we can cultivate a deeper understanding of ourselves and the world around us, leading to enhanced fulfillment, happiness, and inner tranquility.

CHAPTER 19

The Four Pillars of Ikigai: Passion, Mission, Vocation, and Profession

At the heart of Ikigai lies a simple yet profound concept: finding the intersection between what we love, what we are good at, what the world needs, and for what we can be paid. By exploring these four elements, we can discover our true purpose in life and unlock the key to lasting happiness and fulfillment.

Passion

Passion represents what we love to do, the activities and interests that bring us joy and ignite our enthusiasm. By embracing our passions, we can harness a deep-seated source of motivation and energy to propel us toward our goals and dreams. To uncover your passion, ask yourself: What activities make me feel alive and excited? When do I lose track of time because I am so absorbed in what I am doing? For instance, a person who loves to write can start a blog or write a book on a subject they are passionate about, while someone who loves to cook can start a cooking class or create a food blog. These real-life examples demonstrate how embracing one's passions can lead to fulfilling and rewarding pursuits.

Mission

Our mission encompasses how we can use our skills and passions to make a positive difference in the world around us. By identifying our goal, we can find a more profound sense of value and purpose in our lives, knowing that our actions contribute to the greater good. To discover your objective, consider: What problems or challenges do I feel compelled to address? How can I use my skills and talents to create a positive influence in the lives of others? For example, a person who is passionate about the environment can volunteer for a local conservation organization or start a project to reduce waste. Similarly, someone who is interested in mental health can create a support group for individuals struggling with mental health issues. By aligning our skills and passions with a mission to make a positive impact, we can create meaningful change and find purpose in our lives.

Vocation

Vocation refers to our natural talents and abilities, the skills we possess that enable us to excel in particular areas of life. By recognizing and nurturing our attributes, we can achieve a greater sense of mastery and competence, leading to increased satisfaction and self-esteem. To pinpoint your vocation, ask yourself: What am I naturally good at? What activities do I excel in without much effort? For instance, a person who excels in graphic design can work for a design agency or freelance for clients, while someone skilled in coding can follow a calling as a software developer or create their own software company. The key is to identify your innate talents and find ways to apply them in a fulfilling and meaningful way.

Profession

Our profession is the aspect of our lives that provides financial stability and security, enabling us to meet our basic needs and support ourselves and our families. For instance, a person with a passion for fitness can become a personal trainer or start their own gym, which provides financial stability and allows them to pursue their passion for health and wellness. Similarly, someone who loves animals can become a veterinarian or work for an animal rescue organization, creating a fulfilling career that aligns with their passion for animal welfare. By aligning our occupation with our passions, mission, and talents, we can create a more fulfilling and rewarding career path reflecting our true life purpose. To explore the link between your livelihood and your Ikigai, consider: How can I use my skills and passions to create a career that is both financially sustainable and personally fulfilling?

It is important to note that finding one's Ikigai is not a one-time event, but rather a continuous journey of self-discovery and growth. By regularly reflecting on our passions, mission, vocation, and profession, we can continue to align our lives with our true purpose and find fulfillment in the process.

To sum it up, by following the Ikigai framework, we can uncover our true purpose in life and find happiness and fulfillment in all aspects of our lives. It requires a willingness to explore and reflect on our passions, skills, and the needs of the world around us. May this chapter inspire readers to launch on their own journey to discover their Ikigai.

CHAPTER 20
Discovering Your Ikigai

Finding your Ikigai is a deeply personal and transformative trek, requiring introspection, self-awareness, and commitment. By exploring your passions, strengths, values, and goals, you can uncover your true purpose in life and create a more fulfilling and balanced existence.

a. Reflecting on Personal Strengths and Passions

The initial phase in uncovering your Ikigai involves an earnest examination of your strengths, aptitudes, and enthusiasms. Contemplate the pursuits and interests that evoke happiness and gratification in you, and consider the skills and talents that come effortlessly. By acknowledging and incorporating these facets of your personality, you can start to mold a life that better aligns with your intrinsic aspirations and capabilities.

Some questions to consider when reflecting on your strengths and passions include:

— What activities or hobbies do I genuinely enjoy and find fulfilling?
— What tasks or projects do I excel at in my personal and professional life?
— What do others often compliment me on or ask for my help with?

b. Aligning Life Goals with Values and Purpose

Once you have achieved a better awareness of your strengths and passions, you can begin coordinating your life aims with your values and purpose. Afterward, consider how your aptitudes and interests can exert a positive influence on the world around you, and how they correspond with your values and convictions.

To align your life goals with your values and purpose, ask yourself:

— What causes or issues do I feel passionate about or called to address?
— How can I use my strengths and passions to contribute to these causes or issues?
— What short-term and long-term goals can I set for myself to move closer to my Ikigai?

c. Strategies for Cultivating Ikigai in Daily Life

Remember, discovering your Ikigai is a continual process of self-reflection and development. To nurture your Ikigai, consider implementing these strategies into your daily routine:

1. Focus on the present: By becoming more present and conscious of your thoughts, feelings, and experiences, you can gain a greater perspective on inner desires, passions, and purpose.

2. Stay curious: Continually seek new knowledge, experiences, and opportunities to expand your horizons and broaden your world perspective.

3. Develop strong bonds: Cultivate meaningful connections with others who share your values, interests, and goals, and seek opportunities to collaborate, support, and learn from one another.

4. Put yourself first: Ensure that you are taking care of your physical, emotional, and spiritual well-being, as this will provide a solid foundation for pursuing your Ikigai.

5. Establish attainable objectives: Break down your larger life goals into smaller, more manageable steps to make meaningful progress and celebrate achievements along the way. This approach allows you to achieve your objectives while maintaining your motivation and sense of accomplishment.

Discovering your Ikigai is a powerful process that can profoundly transform your life—by reflecting on your strengths, aligning your goals with your values and purpose, and adopting strategies to cultivate your Ikigai daily. I encourage you to embark on this path of self-discovery, to embrace your passions and talents, and to seek opportunities to make a positive difference in the world around you. Finding your Ikigai is a lifelong expedition of self-reflection and growth. So embrace this journey with an open heart and an open mind, and allow the beauty of your Ikigai to reveal itself to you over time.

conclusion.

The Interconnectedness of Wabi-Sabi, Kaizen, and Ikigai

The Impact of Embracing These Philosophies on Overall Well-Being

A Call to Action: Integrating Wabi-Sabi, Kaizen, and Ikigai Into Daily Life for a More Fulfilled, Meaningful Existence

CONCLUSION

The Interconnectedness of Wabi-Sabi, Kaizen, and Ikigai

CONCLUSION | 121

As we reach the conclusion of our exploration of the Japanese philosophies of Wabi-Sabi, Kaizen, and Ikigai, it is important to recognize their interconnectedness and how they can work together to create a more balanced, fulfilling, and purpose-driven life.

Wabi-Sabi, the appreciation of the beauty in imperfection, teaches us to embrace the impermanence and flaws of life, fostering a sense of mindfulness and acceptance. By incorporating Wabi-Sabi into our daily lives, we can learn to appreciate the natural, unadorned beauty surrounding us and within ourselves, cultivating a sense of inner peace and contentment.

Kaizen, the art of continuous improvement, inspires us to consistently seek growth and development in our personal and professional endeavors. By adopting the principles of Kaizen, we can maintain a growth mindset, allowing us to overcome challenges, learn from our mistakes, and continually refine our skills and abilities.

Ikigai, the reason for being, helps us discover our true purpose by identifying the intersection between our passions, strengths, values, and goals. By pursuing our Ikigai, we can create a life that is more closely aligned with our inner desires and potential, fostering greater happiness, fulfillment, and inner harmony.

When combined, these three philosophies create a robust structure for living a more balanced, purposeful, and authentic life. By embracing the principles of Wabi-Sabi, Kaizen, and Ikigai, we can learn to appreciate the beauty of the present moment, continually strive for growth and improvement, and discover our true purpose in life.

As you embark on your own journey of self-discovery and personal growth, I encourage you to reflect on the lessons and insights offered by these ancient Japanese philosophies. By incorporating Wabi-Sabi, Kaizen, and Ikigai into your daily life, you can unlock the secrets to a more fulfilling, joyful, and purpose-driven existence.

The Impact of Embracing These Philosophies on Overall Well-Being

The philosophies of Wabi-Sabi, Kaizen, and Ikigai can potentially transform our individual lives and our overall well-being. When we embrace these philosophies, we can experience a wide range of benefits that touch upon various aspects of our mental, emotional, and physical health.

Mental Well-being:

By adopting the principles of Wabi-Sabi, we can develop a greater sense of mindfulness and acceptance, which can help reduce stress, anxiety, and rumination. As we learn to appreciate the present moment and the appeal of irregularity, we cultivate a sense of tranquility and satisfaction that can contribute to a more balanced mental state.

Similarly, the practice of Kaizen and the pursuit of continuous improvement can foster an expansion mentality and resilience, allowing us to face life's challenges with greater confidence and adaptability. By embracing the process of lifelong learning and self-improvement, we can strengthen our mental resilience and enhance our overall cognitive health.

Emotional Well-being:

The pursuit of Ikigai, or our reason for being, can significantly impact our emotional well-being by providing us with a sense of purpose and direction in life. When we feel connected to our passions and purpose, we are more likely to experience positive emotions such as joy, satisfaction, and fulfillment. This sense of purpose can also serve as a buffer against feelings of loneliness, despair, and hopelessness.

The appreciation of Wabi-Sabi can also contribute to our emotional well-being as we learn to let go of unrealistic expectations and perfectionism, which can be significant sources of emotional distress. By embracing life's shortcomings and promoting a sense of gratitude, we can create more positive emotional states and improve our overall emotional health.

Physical Well-being:

Embracing the principles of Kaizen, Wabi-Sabi, and Ikigai can indirectly bolster our physical well-being by inspiring healthier lifestyle choices and habits. For example, when prioritizing self-improvement and personal growth, we are more likely to incorporate behaviors supporting our physical health, such as regular exercise, a balanced diet, and sufficient sleep. Furthermore, the stress reduction and emotional stability that can result from conducting these notions may lead to improved immune function, reduced inflammation, and a lower risk of chronic diseases.

The effect of internalizing the teachings of Wabi-Sabi, Kaizen, and Ikigai on our holistic well-being is noteworthy. By infusing these principles into our daily routine, we can achieve better mental, emotional, and physical health, resulting in a more harmonious, rewarding, and purposeful existence.

A Call to Action: Integrating Wabi-Sabi, Kaizen, and Ikigai into Daily Life for a More Fulfilled, Meaningful Existence

As we have explored throughout this book, the philosophies of Wabi-Sabi, Kaizen, and Ikigai can offer priceless wisdom and direction on the journey toward a more fulfilled, meaningful life. By embodying these concepts and blending them into our daily habits, we can create persistent positive change and cultivate an elevated sense of purpose, happiness, and well-being. With this in mind, I invite you to take action and begin your expedition of self-discovery and personal growth.

Here are some useful techniques to help you integrate Wabi-Sabi, Kaizen, and Ikigai into your daily life:

Practice self-compassion
Treat yourself with kindness, understanding, and forgiveness when you make mistakes or face setbacks, embracing the Wabi-Sabi philosophy of accepting imperfection.

Embrace change
Develop a flexible and adaptable mindset, welcoming change, and new experiences as opportunities for growth and alignment with the Wabi-Sabi, Kaizen, and Ikigai principles.

Focus on quality over quantity
Prioritize quality in your work and relationships, aligning with the Wabi-Sabi and Kaizen philosophies emphasizing depth, meaning, and genuine connection.

Seek inspiration
Curate and surround yourself with sources of inspiration that align with the principles of Wabi-Sabi, Kaizen, and Ikigai, such as art, literature, or mentorship.

Develop emotional intelligence
Enhance your ability to recognize, comprehend, and manage your emotions, as well as empathize with the feelings of others.

Find joy in simplicity
Simplify your life by decluttering your physical surroundings and focusing on the activities and relationships that truly matter to you.

Remain open to new experiences and opportunities
Explore new ideas, perspectives, and experiences that can enrich your life and deepen your understanding of yourself and the world around you.

Create balance
Work towards achieving equilibrium in all aspects of your life, including professional life, relationships, and personal pursuits, to maintain a sense of harmony and wellness.

CONCLUSION

As we reach the end of this exploration into the extraordinary philosophies of Wabi-Sabi, Kaizen, and Ikigai, it is evident that these concepts, deeply rooted in Japanese culture, offer us a wealth of wisdom and guidance. Furthermore, by recognizing the interconnectedness of these ideologies, we can discover new ways to approach life and instill a habit of continuous growth, self-improvement, and appreciation for the charm of imperfect beauty surrounding us.

The transformative impact of embracing Wabi-Sabi, Kaizen, and Ikigai on our overall well-being is truly phenomenal. By incorporating these philosophies into our daily routines, we can achieve better mental, emotional, and physical health, leading to a more meaningful, rewarding, and purposeful existence.

The journey does not end here, though. The real transformation begins when we apply these teachings to our everyday lives. So, I invite you, dear reader, to embark on a transformative path of self-discovery and personal evolution by integrating the principles of Wabi-Sabi, Kaizen, and Ikigai into your life. Start by celebrating imperfection in all its forms, cultivating a growth-oriented mentality, and identifying your passion, whether in your personal or professional pursuits.

Now that we have explored the core principles of Wabi-Sabi, Kaizen, and Ikigai, it is time for you to take this knowledge and apply it to your own life. In the glossary of Japanese terms, you will find additional concepts and ideas that can further deepen your understanding of these philosophies. As a bonus, I have also included practical tips for incorporating Wabi-Sabi, Kaizen, and Ikigai into your daily routines, making it easier for you to integrate these powerful principles into your life. By doing so, you can gradually incorporate these powerful principles into your life, and over time, witness the transformative effects they can have on your overall well-being and sense of purpose.

As you set foot on this journey of self-exploration and inner growth, remember that true transformation begins when you take the teachings of Wabi-Sabi, Kaizen, and Ikigai to heart and put them into practice. By choosing to accept the allures of imperfection, prioritizing lifelong learning, and aligning your actions with your deepest values and passions, you can build a life filled with meaning and direction, while encouraging others to do likewise.

In conclusion, I encourage you, dear reader, to take this wisdom to heart and apply it to your daily life. The powerful teachings of Wabi-Sabi, Kaizen, and Ikigai await you, offering the opportunity for profound transformation and growth. Let us all embrace these principles and create a world in which each individual lives with a deep sense of purpose, cultivates a mindset of development and improvement, and appreciates the transient beauty that life has to offer.

appendices

Glossary of Japanese Terms

Bonus Tips for Incorporating Wabi-Sabi, Kaizen, and Ikigai into Daily Routines

Glossary of Japanese Terms

A

Andon (アンドン)
A Japanese term that refers to a system used in manufacturing or production processes to signal when an abnormality has occurred. It typically involves a visual signal, such as a light or a display board, to indicate the location and nature of the problem, allowing workers to quickly address the issue and prevent it from causing further problems.

B

Blue Zone
Areas of the world where people live exceptionally long and healthy lives. These zones align with the principles of Ikigai and Kaizen, as they prioritize purposeful living, healthy habits, and continuous self-improvement.

Buddhism (仏教):
A religion and philosophy that originated in ancient India and is practiced in many parts of the world, including Japan. It shares principles with Wabi-Sabi, Kaizen, and Ikigai, such as the pursuit of inner peace, personal growth, and a focus on the present moment.

Bushido (武士道)
The way of the samurai, a code of conduct and moral principles adhered to by the samurai warriors of feudal Japan. It emphasizes virtues such as loyalty, honor, courage, and self-discipline, aligning with the principles of Kaizen and Ikigai.

C

Chanoyu (茶の湯), Chado (茶道), or Sado (茶道)
The way of the samurai, a code of conduct and moral principles adhered to by the samurai warriors of feudal Japan. It emphasizes virtues such as loyalty, honor, courage, and self-discipline, aligning with the principles of Kaizen and Ikigai.

F

Fukinsei (不均整)
A Japanese aesthetic principle that embraces the beauty of asymmetry and irregularity. It aligns with the Wabi-Sabi philosophy by valuing imperfection and the natural flow of life.

G

Ganbatte (頑張って)
A Japanese expression meaning "do your best" or "keep going," often used as a form of encouragement and to show moral support.

Genki (元気)
A Japanese word meaning energetic, lively, or healthy, often used to describe a person's physical or mental state. It can be associated with the concepts of Ikigai and Kaizen, as it implies a sense of well-being and a continuous effort to improve oneself.

Gemba (現場)
A Japanese term meaning "the actual place" or "the real place." It is used in a business context to refer to the location where the work is being done.

H

Hansei (反省)
A Japanese word meaning self-reflection and introspection, typically in the context of personal growth, improvement, and acceptance of imperfection.

Hara hachi bu (腹八分目):
An Okinawan principle that encourages eating until you are 80% full, promoting moderation and healthy eating habits. By practicing Hara hachi bu, it is believed that individuals can maintain a healthy weight, improve digestion, and reduce the risk of health problems associated with overeating.

Hatarakigai" (働きがい)
A Japanese term that means "work worth doing" and is closely related to the concept of Ikigai. It emphasizes finding purpose and fulfillment in one's work by aligning it with one's passions and values.

I

Ikigai (生き甲斐):
A Japanese concept that represents the "reason for being" or "one's purpose in life," found at the intersection of passion, mission, vocation, and profession, the things that give individuals a sense of fulfillment and a meaningful life.

K

Kaizen (改善):
The philosophy of continuous improvement, emphasizing incremental progress and growth in both personal and professional aspects of life. It involves identifying areas for improvement, setting goals, and regularly reviewing and adjusting practices to achieve those goals

Kanban (看板)
A term that refers to a visual system for managing work processes and inventory using cards, boards, or other visual aids to signal the need for and progress of work tasks.

Kanso (簡素):
A Japanese aesthetic principle that values simplicity, clarity, and the elimination of clutter. It aligns with Kaizen's continuous improvement philosophy and Wabi-Sabi's appreciation for the beauty of natural simplicity and imperfection.

Keshiki (景色):
Refers to the natural landscapes or scenery in Japan that are appreciated for their aesthetic beauty and simplicity, embodying the principles of Wabi-Sabi, and promoting a sense of mindfulness and connection to nature.

Kintsugi (金継ぎ)
The Japanese artistry of repairing broken pottery with gold or other precious metals, embracing imperfections, and highlighting the object's history as part of its beauty.

Koh-do (香道)
Traditional Japanese art of incense appreciation, which involves the use of natural incense materials to create a meditative and sensory experience. It relates to the principles of Wabi-Sabi and Kaizen by promoting mindfulness, simplicity, and the pursuit of continuous improvement in one's sensory experiences.

Kominka (古民家)
Refers to traditional Japanese houses that have been renovated and modernized while preserving their original character and design. This aligns with the Wabi-Sabi philosophy by valuing the beauty of imperfection and the natural materials used in the construction, and with the Kaizen philosophy by promoting continuous improvement in preserving and maintaining these historic structures.

M

Ma (間)
Refers to the space between objects, events, or moments, and the perception of that space. In the context of Wabi-Sabi, it emphasizes the beauty of negative space and the importance of simplicity. It also aligns with the philosophy of Kaizen, encouraging constant evaluation and improvement of the distances between objects or events to optimize efficiency and harmony.

Moai (模合)
A traditional Japanese social group emphasizing mutual support, cooperation, and community building. This concept aligns with the principles of Ikigai, as moai groups promote a sense of belonging, purpose, and connection to others.

Mono no aware (物の哀れ)
A Japanese concept that refers to the awareness and appreciation of the impermanence and fleeting nature of life.

Mottainai (もったいない)
A Japanese term conveying the feeling of regret for waste or the underutilization of resources, often used to encourage conservation and environmentalism. It also embodies the idea of mindful living and sustainability, aligning with the cherishing of resources and reducing excess in Wabi-Sabi.

Muda (無駄)
A Japanese term that means waste or futility, referring to any activity that consumes resources without adding value.

Mujō (無常):
Japanese term that refers to the impermanence and transience of life. This concept is aligned with the Wabi-Sabi philosophy, which embraces the beauty of imperfection and the ephemerality of all things.

N

Noh (能)
A traditional Japanese theatrical performance that embodies the principles of Kaizen through its meticulous attention to detail and continuous refinement. The art form features slow, stylized movements, music, dance, and drama and often employs masks for heightened expression.

O

Omotenashi (おもてなし)
The Japanese approach to hospitality, emphasizing anticipatory and attentive service, ensuring that guests feel genuinely welcomed and cared for. It aligns with Ikigai, which involves finding joy and purpose in serving and pleasing others.

R

Ryokans (旅館)
Traditional Japanese inns that provide a unique cultural experience for guests through their emphasis on hospitality, nature, and simplicity, reflecting the principles of Wabi-Sabi and Ikigai.

S

Sabi (寂):
A concept in Wabi-Sabi philosophy that represents the beauty found in the passage of time and the impermanent nature of all things. It is typically associated with objects or places that exhibit a weathered, rustic quality and evoke a sense of melancholy or nostalgia.

Samurai (侍):
A member of a powerful military nobility of medieval and early modern Japan, known for their code of honor and loyalty, called Bushido. The principles of Bushido align with the values of Kaizen and Ikigai, emphasizing the pursuit of personal improvement and a sense of purpose in one's actions.

GLOSSARY OF JAPANESE TERMS

Sashiko (刺し子)
A traditional form of Japanese embroidery that involves stitching geometric patterns with white cotton thread on indigo fabric, reflecting the Wabi-Sabi philosophy of finding beauty in imperfection through the process of continuous improvement (Kaizen) and the pursuit of a meaningful and purposeful life (Ikigai).

Seijaku (静寂)
The concept of finding tranquility and stillness within the chaos of daily life, usually seen in Zen Buddhism and meditation. It is often associated with the idea of mindfulness and the ability to find inner peace in the present moment.

Shibui (渋い)
A Japanese term that refers to a simple, subtle, and unobtrusive beauty that can be found in objects, designs, or behaviors. It is typically associated with minimalism, elegance, and understated refinement.

Shikata ga nai (仕方がない)
A Japanese expression that means "it cannot be helped" or "there is no other way," typically used to accept and move on from difficult or uncontrollable situations. While it may seem defeatist, it can also be seen as a reminder to embrace the impermanence and acceptance of the present moment, which aligns with the principles of Wabi-Sabi and Ikigai.

Shinrin-yoku (森林浴)
A Japanese practice that translates to "forest bathing," which involves immersing oneself in nature and the forest environment to promote well-being. It relates to the concept of Ikigai, emphasizing the importance of connecting with nature and finding purpose and meaning in life.

Shintoism (神道)
An Indigenous religion of Japan that emphasizes the harmonious connection between humans and nature. Its focus on purity, gratitude, and respect for the natural world aligns with the values of Wabi-Sabi, Kaizen, and Ikigai.

Shizen (自然):
Refers to the natural state of things and is in harmony with the philosophy of Wabi-Sabi, valuing the beauty found in simplicity and imperfection. It also relates to Ikigai in that it emphasizes living in harmony with one's environment and finding purpose in natural pursuits.

Shokunin (職人)
An expression that refers to a highly skilled artisan who embodies the principles of lifelong learning, continuous improvement, and dedication to their craft. The term emphasizes technical proficiency and an attitude of dedication, commitment, and constant improvement.

GLOSSARY OF JAPANESE TERMS | 135

Sumi-e (墨絵)
A traditional Japanese painting technique that uses black ink to create delicate and minimalistic brushstroke images. It aligns with the principles of Wabi-Sabi by celebrating imperfection and simplicity, and supports the pursuit of Ikigai by providing a meditative and introspective activity.

Wabi (侘)
A Japanese term that refers to a sense of quiet simplicity and subdued elegance, often characterized by rustic and natural elements. It is a central concept in the Wabi-Sabi philosophy, which emphasizes finding beauty in imperfection and appreciating the transient nature of all things.

Wabi-Sabi (侘び寂び)
A Japanese philosophy that celebrates the beauty of imperfection and impermanence, emphasizing simplicity, humility, and authenticity.

Yakimono (焼き物)
Japanese word for pottery, which is considered an art form that embodies the principles of Wabi-Sabi, Kaizen, and Ikigai. Through the creation process, potters strive for continuous improvement, finding joy and purpose in their craft and embracing the imperfections that make each piece unique.

Yūgen (幽玄)
An aesthetic concept that refers to a profound and mysterious sense of beauty that is beyond intellectual understanding, often characterized by subtle and understated elegance and complexity.

Yutori (ゆとり)
A Japanese term that refers to the concept of spaciousness and the need for balance in life. It relates to the philosophy of Ikigai and highlights the significance of discovering a feeling of ease and fulfillment in daily life, rather than being constantly rushed or stressed.

Z

Zen (禅)
A school of Mahayana Buddhism that emphasizes meditation and mindfulness to attain spiritual awakening. It connects to Wabi-Sabi, Kaizen, and Ikigai through its teachings on simplicity, impermanence, and the appreciation of the present moment, which form the foundation of these Japanese philosophies.

Bonus Tips for Incorporating Wabi-Sabi, Kaizen, and Ikigai into Daily Routines

Incorporating the philosophies of Wabi-Sabi, Kaizen, and Ikigai into your daily routines can help you cultivate a more balanced, fulfilling, and purposeful life. Here are some practical tips for integrating these concepts into your everyday activities:

01 Morning Reflection:
Begin each day with a brief moment of reflection, considering your personal values, goals, and passions. An example could be taking a few minutes before starting your day to meditate, write in your journal, or simply sit in silence and organize your thoughts for the day ahead. This practice can help you stay focused on your Ikigai and prioritize your tasks to approach them with a sense of clarity and purpose.

02 Mindful Eating
Practice mindful eating by savoring each bite, appreciating the flavors and textures of your food, and eating until you are 80% full (Hara hachi bu). This approach embodies the principles of Wabi-Sabi and Kaizen by promoting mindfulness, moderation, and gratitude. By focusing on the sensory experience of eating, you can increase your enjoyment and satisfaction of your meal and make more conscious choices about what you eat. For example, instead of mindlessly snacking on chips while watching TV, you could savor a piece of fruit and appreciate its taste, texture, and aroma. This approach aligns with the principles of Wabi-Sabi and Kaizen by promoting awareness, moderation, and gratitude in daily life.

03 Daily Journaling

Keep a daily journal to record your thoughts, feelings, and experiences. This practice can help you track your personal growth, identify areas for improvement, and maintain a focus on your Ikigai. For example, you could set aside a few minutes each evening to reflect on your day and write down any insights or lessons learned. This simple practice can help you gain clarity and perspective on your life and promote personal growth and fulfillment.

04 Set Small, Achievable Goals

Break down larger objectives into smaller, more manageable tasks, and celebrate your progress along the way. This approach aligns with the Kaizen philosophy of continuous improvement and can help you maintain momentum toward your goals. For instance, if you aspire to run a marathon, you might start by running a mile a day and gradually increasing the distance over time. This approach allows you to build up your endurance and confidence while tracking your progress and celebrating your accomplishments along the way.

05 Cultivate Gratitude

Practice gratitude by regularly acknowledging the things you appreciate in your life. This practice can help you embrace the Wabi-Sabi mindset of finding beauty in imperfection and enjoying the now. The simple act of thanking those who help or support you can cultivate a sense of gratitude in your daily life. Whether expressing your appreciation in person or through a thoughtful message, by acknowledging the positive influences in your life, you can shift your focus to the present moment and find joy in the small things.

06 Engage in Mindful Activities

Incorporate activities such as yoga, meditation, or deep breathing exercises into your daily routine to promote mindfulness and reduce stress. These practices can support your pursuit of Wabi-Sabi, Kaizen, and Ikigai by creating a greater sense of presence and awareness. For example, taking a few minutes each morning to practice deep breathing exercises can help you approach the day with a calmer and more focused mindset, allowing you to tackle tasks with greater efficiency and intention.

07 Create an Organized, Clutter-Free Environment

Apply the 5S methodology (Sort, Set in order, Shine, Standardize, Sustain) to maintain a clean and organized living space. This practice supports the principles of Kaizen and can help you create an environment that facilitates productivity, focus, and well-being. For example, by organizing your desk according to the 5S principles, you can reduce distractions and increase efficiency when working.

08 Nurture Relationships

Make time for meaningful connections with friends, family, and loved ones, as these relationships can contribute to your sense of Ikigai and overall happiness. An example would be regularly scheduling a coffee date with a close friend, or setting aside time for a weekly phone call with a family member can help strengthen these connections and contribute to your overall well-being.

Pursue Lifelong Learning
Engage in continuous learning and personal development through reading, attending workshops, or taking courses in areas that interest you. This practice aligns with the Kaizen philosophy and can lead to both personal and professional growth. For instance, learning a new language, taking a cooking class, or studying a new subject can help you broaden your horizons and discover new passions.

Embrace Imperfection
Practice acceptance and compassion for yourself and others, recognizing that everyone has unique strengths and weaknesses. This mindset is central to the philosophy of Wabi-Sabi and can help you cultivate a more balanced and accepting approach to life. For instance, instead of beating yourself up for making a mistake at work, you can approach it as a valuable learning experience and move forward with a positive attitude.

Develop a Morning and Evening Routine:
Establishing routines can help you create a sense of order and purpose in your daily life. For example, you could start your day with a brief moment of reflection or gratitude, followed by a few minutes of stretching or meditation. Then, at night, review your day and plan your next steps. Reflecting on your progress and areas for improvement can also help you maintain momentum and stay aligned with your purpose.

Practice Active Listening:
Enhance your communication and relationships by practicing active listening. This approach, which involves fully focusing on the speaker and providing empathetic responses, aligns with the principles of Kaizen and Ikigai by promoting understanding, compassion, and connection.

Embrace Nature

Spend time in nature to appreciate its beauty and imperfections, a practice that aligns with the Wabi-Sabi philosophy. Nature can also provide a space for reflection and introspection, supporting your pursuit of Ikigai. Find a local park or nature trail to walk, hike, or bike and make it a regular part of your routine. Being surrounded by nature can help reduce stress and anxiety and promote feelings of calm and well-being.

Cultivate Patience

Practicing patience in your daily life, both with yourself and others, can profoundly affect your overall wellness and relationship with others. One example of this is when interacting with difficult individuals, as it can be tempting to respond with frustration or anger. However, maintaining a compassionate and empathetic perspective can lead to more positive outcomes and strengthen your connections with others. Additionally, this approach aligns with the principles of Wabi-Sabi and Kaizen, as it promotes acceptance, kindness, and a focus on incremental progress. By embracing the practice of patience, you can establish a greater sense of inner peace and understanding, leading to a more fulfilling and purposeful life.

Prioritize Self-Care

Make self-care a regular part of your daily routine, attending to your physical, emotional, and spiritual needs. It involves making time for activities that nourish your mind and body, such as exercise, healthy eating, restful sleep, and engaging in hobbies or interests. This approach also involves setting healthy boundaries and learning to say no to activities that may not align with your well-being. For instance, setting aside time for a relaxing bath or engaging in meditation or yoga can help reduce stress and promote a sense of calm. Moreover, cultivating self-compassion and utilizing positive self-talk can help improve your emotional well-being and promote a positive mindset. By prioritizing self-care, you can build a strong foundation for personal growth and fulfillment, which aligns with the pursuit of Ikigai.

16 Seek Feedback

By inviting constructive criticism from others, you can gain insights into your strengths and weaknesses and identify areas for improvement. This aligns with the Kaizen philosophy of continuous improvement, where small, incremental changes can lead to considerable progress over time. Additionally, being open to feedback demonstrates a willingness to learn and grow, which can help you build stronger relationships and foster a culture of collaboration and innovation. To illustrate, if you are working on a project, you could seek feedback from colleagues or supervisors to improve your work. This feedback could help you refine your ideas, detect weak points, and ultimately produce a better end product. Similarly, if you seek personal development, you could ask a trusted friend or mentor for feedback on your communication style or other areas where you want to improve. Their constructive criticism can help you understand your strengths and weaknesses and guide you toward incredible personal growth.

17 Schedule Regular Reflection Time

Regular reflection time is an effective way to check in with yourself and assess whether you are on track with your personal goals and values. By dedicating time to introspection and self-evaluation, you can gain a clearer understanding of your strengths, weaknesses, and areas for improvement. This practice also aligns with the principles of Wabi-Sabi, Kaizen, and Ikigai by promoting mindfulness, self-awareness, and continuous improvement. For instance, you could schedule 30 minutes at the end of each week to reflect on the past seven days. During this time, you might review your progress toward your goals, evaluate your time management and productivity, and consider any challenges you face. Based on your reflection, you could adjust your approach for the upcoming week by setting new priorities or modifying your routines to better support your goals. By regularly scheduling time for self-reflection and adjustment, you can maintain a sense of focus and purpose in your daily life.

Volunteer and Give Back

Engage in volunteer work or other acts of service, as these activities can contribute to your sense of purpose and Ikigai. For example, volunteering at a local shelter or food bank can benefit those in need and provide you with a sense of satisfaction and connection to the community. You could also consider participating in a beach or park clean-up, organizing a fundraiser for a cause you care about, or offering your time and skills to a non-profit organization. In addition to the benefits of helping others, volunteering can also provide personal benefits, such as the opportunity to develop new skills, gain experience, and make new connections. It can also help you gain a new perspective on life and appreciate what you have.

Create Art or Engage in Creative Hobbies

Engaging in creative hobbies or creating art can be a therapeutic way to express oneself, allowing you to relax and unwind. Whether it's painting, writing, sculpting, or any other creative outlet, these activities can provide a sense of purpose and fulfillment, aligning with the principles of Ikigai. These pursuits can also help you appreciate the beauty of imperfection, as you explore innovative ideas and experiment with different techniques. For example, creating a painting or writing a poem can help you process complex emotions and acquire a more in-depth understanding of your experiences. Similarly, gardening can provide a space for reflection and connection with nature, as you tend to your plants and observe their growth and development over time. By incorporating creative pursuits into your life, you can align with the principles of Wabi-Sabi and find new productive ways to connect with yourself and the world around you.

20. Surround Yourself with Positive Influences

By intentionally curating your environment to include uplifting books, inspiring art, and supportive individuals who share your values and goals, you create a space that promotes positivity and growth. For instance, if you are striving to incorporate the principles of Wabi-Sabi into your life, you might decorate your space with natural and imperfect elements, such as plants or handmade pottery. Additionally, surrounding yourself with individuals who share your values and goals can provide you with support, encouragement, and accountability. By adopting this approach, you can uphold your enthusiasm and stay on track toward maintaining motivation, focus, and a positive mindset.

As you embrace these practical tips and weave them into your daily routines, you set the stage for the powerful and transformative philosophies of Wabi-Sabi, Kaizen, and Ikigai to infuse your life. Remember, these philosophies are not one-size-fits-all solutions, but rather a starting point for self-discovery and personal growth. May this journey of exploration and integration bring you joy, wisdom, and a deeper connection to yourself and the world around you. Until next time.

www.ingramcontent.com/pod-product-compliance
Lightning Source LLC
Chambersburg PA
CBHW051614010526
44107CB00036B/1422/J